First Steps out of Depression

Why this book?

You might have picked up this bo[ok to]
help you because:

- you feel desperately sad and confused;
- life feels out of control;
- the fear is intolerable.

You search around for help, but you are just told to:

- pull yourself together;
- count your blessings;
- get a grip and get on with life.

If only it were that easy!

Maybe you don't want to admit you need help. You might think...

- My family needs me. I must keep going.
- If I'm honest about how I feel, I might lose my job.

It could be that you are experiencing depression. And, yes: you need help. This book will enable you to take the first steps towards getting your life back.

For David, Jonathan, and Rachel.
You have given me more joy than I can ever express.
Thank you.

First Steps out of Depression

Sue Atkinson

LION

Copyright © 2010 Sue Atkinson
This edition copyright © 2010 Lion Hudson
The author asserts the moral right
to be identified as the author of this work

A Lion Book
an imprint of
Lion Hudson plc
Wilkinson House, Jordan Hill Road,
Oxford OX2 8DR, England
www.lionhudson.com
ISBN 978 0 7459 5513 1

Distributed by:
UK: Marston Book Services, PO Box 269,
Abingdon, Oxon, OX14 4YN
USA: Trafalgar Square Publishing, 814
N. Franklin Street, Chicago, IL 60610
USA Christian Market: Kregel Publications,
PO Box 2607, Grand Rapids, MI 49501
First edition 2010
10 9 8 7 6 5 4 3 2 1 0
All rights reserved

A catalogue record for this book is available
from the British Library
Typeset in 10/12 ITC Stone Serif
Printed and bound in Malta

Contents

Acknowledgments

I want to thank all those people who have contributed towards this book. Some have known they were helping me with my research, but others have just been sharing their journey with me in conversations and during my workshops. All of this has enabled me to have a deeper understanding of our first steps out of depression.

I particularly want to thank the young man in one of my workshops who got as fed up as I was with some people being negative about ways we can get out of depression. He said vehemently, "Depression is utterly awful. Let's get out of here!" I've incorporated his great thought into this book.

A special thank you to my friends in Mulbarton, Norfolk, especially Lynne Lambert and Anne Mary Stubenbord, and the Depression Support Group who helped me enormously in the early stages of this book.

Many people in the UK charity Depression Alliance have supported and encouraged me for many years, especially Judy and Paul Lanham, and Maggy Clode whose friendship has meant so much to me.

Thank you.
Sue Atkinson
London, January 2010

Introduction

Depression will affect about one in every four or five people at some point. This means that it is much more common than we might think, and in everyone's circle of family and friends, there are almost certainly several people who have experienced it.

Given how common depression is, it's odd that it isn't talked about all that much. So when it hits us, we can feel lonely, abandoned, and ashamed. We desperately don't want the label "mentally ill"!

Things we need to know about depression

- Depression can affect anyone – rich, poor, brilliant sports person, child, politician, doctor, celebrity – and those we think must be happy and contented with their life.
- Some people can be more prone to depression than others. (Apparently it can sometimes be genetic.)
- Depression is an illness. Just as we might need to take medication for thyroid problems or diabetes, so we might need to take antidepressants to lift us out of the darkness.
- Our body chemistry changes and this is why depression is often helped by taking medication.

> • There seems to be no single cause of depression. It seems to be a mixture of many different things, from what has happened in our life in the past, to what we think about ourselves in the present.

What are the signs or symptoms of depression?

Depression can be very mild and you may feel you only have one or more of these symptoms. But it can also be so severe that it is life-threatening.

Physical signs

- Sleep problems such as waking really early or needing to sleep much more than usual.
- Exhaustion or "burnout".
- Agitation or restlessness.
- Changes in eating, either eating too much or too little, and maybe an obsession with weight.
- Feeling really awful at particular times of the day – often the early morning.
- Bursting into tears at the slightest thing.

Feelings

- Feeling an overwhelming sense of unexplained sadness and hopelessness.
- Feeling upset, fearful, worthless, guilty, ashamed or so numb we feel nothing.
- Losing interest in things we used to enjoy: hill-walking, sex, reading, going to films, etc. All these now seem dull and boring, and we don't have the will or energy to do any of them.
- Feeling alone even when we are in a crowd.

First Steps out of Depression

Thoughts

- Unable to concentrate or focus on things.
- Thinking everything is hopeless.
- Losing confidence in ourselves.
- Thinking, "I hate myself."
- Expecting the worst to happen.
- Thinking people hate us.
- Thinking about killing ourselves.

If you are having suicidal thoughts, get help today.
- Ring a helpline. (See the Useful Resources section at the back of this book.)
- Go and see your doctor.
- Tell someone you trust.

Suicide is a tragic, permanent solution to a temporary problem that will go away once your depression lifts.

Remember:
- Depression ends. It feels as if it won't, but it will.
- You will get better.
- But you need help.

Getting help

Reading this book will help you to take steps away from depression, but you are likely also to need to do the following:

- Go to see your doctor. He or she might be able to suggest some face-to-face help – although waiting lists for counselling and therapy can be long.

- Talk to your doctor about whether you need some kind of medication. This can help us to feel OK enough to work out what's keeping us depressed. I find antidepressants very helpful indeed.

- Start a notebook or journal. Talking and writing are important to our recovery and I strongly recommend them. Just scribbling a few words can have an amazingly helpful effect.

Mythbuster

There are rather a lot of myths about depression. Here is one of them. You will find other examples as you read through the book.

If I go to the doctor and she says I'm depressed that means I'm mentally ill. My family will reject me and I'll never get another job.

Yes, some people might reject us, but lots won't – and gradually employers are grasping the idea that being depressed doesn't mean a person can't work.

My first experience of depression

My first Big D was when I was fourteen. Of course, I had no idea what was happening to me, and I suspect that those around me at school and at home thought it was just teenage angst.

But I was devastated with the sense of alienation from everything. It was unutterably awful and, to my horror, these feelings have come back many times in my life. (But some people only get depressed once.) Eventually, with the help of kind doctors, I worked out that these hideous feelings are depression.

A journey

Also when I was fourteen, at school we read a unique story, *The Pilgrim's Progress*, written by John Bunyan when he was in prison in the seventeenth century.

I was fascinated by the journey that the pilgrim struggled with. He was trying to get himself out of the "slough of despond", which I pictured in my mind as a sludgy bog of quicksand that would suck me in if I didn't put my energy into escaping from it.

The pilgrim was accosted at all times by many people and situations that got in the way of his journey. But each time he had a setback, he found the strength to get himself together again and plod on.

This has been my experience over many years of depression. Gradually it is possible to take steps to get beyond it. Back in my teenage years I had absolutely no idea what those first steps were. But having survived many depressions, I've worked out what helps to get out of the gloom to somewhere more comfortable.

Making decisions

I've found that when I'm depressed I can't even make simple decisions such as which kind of sandwich I want for lunch! But although these everyday choices are difficult, there are some deeply "life-changing" issues that we need (gently) to start to consider.

So in this book I've visualized this as us needing to choose between a "negative" pathway (for example, letting ourselves go on and on thinking about some bad thing that has happened) or choosing a more positive path (for example, working at stopping that ruminating and focusing instead on beautiful creative things).

First steps out of depression

Being depressed has been described in many different ways:

- a dark pit;
- being inside a bell jar;
- standing at the foot of a cliff with vertical sides and no handholds.

Whatever picture of depression you have in your mind of your deep sadness, we probably all agree that it is:

- painful and lonely;
- so awful we want to escape;
- the worst thing we've ever faced in our life.

We definitely don't want to stay in this abysmal place. So *let's get out of here*, one small step at a time.

1

Staying in bed vs. Grabbing the moment

One aspect of depression that most people experience is that they wish to stay in bed (or hide from the pressures of life in some way) and have no incentive to do anything.

- "What's the point of getting up anyway? It'll be an awful day, just like yesterday."

- "I just can't face the world."

- "I'm hopeless at everything so people are better off without me there."

We need to be clear that *there are times when a depressed person needs to stay in bed.* There can be a genuine need to rest – sometimes for days. But once that time is over, it can become counterproductive to go on hiding away.

How do we tell when we need to stop the resting and get up? The answer is: with great difficulty!

What people say...
"I just watch the television all day. That's all I do."
   Arthur, aged 69, retired engineer

I wonder if I could get up?

One of the most crucial skills to learn on our journey away from depression is to do something the instant that a positive thought enters our mind.

So if you are lying in bed and think, "Hmm, I think I might switch the radio on," then *do it immediately*. If you don't grab that moment, it will be gone and you'll lie there for another hour – or the rest of the day. It's just like an alarm clock strategy when you need to catch a train. If you turn the ring off and say, "I'll just rest for another few minutes," you risk dozing off and being late.

I did it

An outcome of getting up and doing at least one thing – perhaps letting the cat out – is that it can add to our sense of getting going. The trick at this point is to congratulate ourselves. OK, that might sound stupid, but as the saying goes, "Nothing succeeds like success."

I make the point, now, of telling myself how well I've done when I've got myself going on mornings when I just want to lie and do nothing. Telling myself I just did something well really does make me feel better.

I have to keep going

Those of us at home with children have no choice but to care for them. There is no option. Be aware that there are at least two important effects of this:

• It is utterly draining of energy – and this has long-term consequences.

- It shows all of us that *we can defeat our feelings* just by keeping going. We *can* grab the moment.

If this applies to you, rest when you can and try to get some practical help, perhaps teaming up with another parent and looking after each other's children sometimes.

Lethargy strikes
But the dreaded lethargy can trap us in that slough of despond for weeks, even months. Arthur, who watches television all day, asked me, "How do I teach myself to switch off the television?"

The only way out of the lethargy of depression is to do it. Switch the television off. *Make yourself do it!*

Understanding our lethargy
There seems to be two main reasons for our total lack of incentive to do anything:

1. Because our body chemistry has changed, there just aren't as many of the good messages going through our brain and this makes us weary. It's not clear whether these changes happen first, then we get depressed, or we get depressed first and that makes the body chemistry change. But the outcome is the same – we are exhausted just thinking about starting the day and we are likely to lie on the sofa and eat badly, making a bad situation even worse.

2. Surprisingly, *what we think* can be making us feel lethargic. Honestly! This is true. *Thinking* negative thoughts makes us *feel* negative.

What people say...
"*Don't be a loner, because isolation has been shown to heighten feelings of failure and lowers ability to cope with stress. It*

also increases vulnerability to viral and bacterial infections by lowering immune system function."

An NHS doctor

Negative thinking

When we're depressed it's all too easy to keep giving ourselves so much "negative feedback" that in effect we're just keeping ourselves in the sinking bog and preventing ourselves getting on with the journey.

We say things like:

- "My life is awful and will never be any different."
- "Everything I do is a disaster."
- "I hate everything about myself."

It's hardly surprising that if we're thinking these things, we'll feel low and anxious. (See Chapter 6 for more detail about negative thinking.)

Not caring I'm a slob

Inevitably being depressed, even mildly, brings with it a sense that everything is just too much to cope with. We start looking for easier options such as eating fast food instead of making a meal with healthy ingredients. Even looking after our body and brushing our hair can become a trial.

Eating badly and making no effort to get exercise can mean that as well as feeling sad, we can start to feel that sense of malaise that comes from eating those vein-clogging trans fats, artificial colourings, and sweeteners that are so bad for our body.

What people say...

"I stand in the kitchen and eat anything I can find. I get pizzas delivered and I've put on five stone... I don't care that I'm obese

and I don't care that my doctor said I'm heading for a heart attack. I'm too depressed to do anything about it."
Gary

What's the point?
We ask ourselves, "What's the point in being healthy? I don't care." And that is a normal reaction in depression.

But, given that the journey to get better from depression is complex, it is a good idea to identify the *easier* first steps.

Easier steps
There isn't much about getting better from depression that is easy, but deciding to make healthy choices is one of the easier first steps.

We don't need to make drastic changes. Little things can all add up to helping our body to feel better.

- Cut down on those unhealthy fats that are in take-away meals by making simple easy meals at home, such as baked beans or poached eggs.

- Eating fruit and veg is one very easy way to improve your diet, as is buying good quality bread and eating tinned fish instead of fat-laden battered fish with chips.

- Cutting down on salt and animal fats in meat and cheese will help to reduce the risk of high blood pressure. (Being depressed is very stressful and that raises our blood pressure. This can lead to strokes.)

Gentle exercise
Just walking downstairs might be the only exercise we get on the days when we feel stuck in the mire, but as we start to heal, a little bit more moving around helps us feel we really are on our journey out of depression.

Don't start running or doing some kind of high-impact sport without seeing your doctor first, especially if you are overweight.

Brisk walking is just great. It burns fat, is easy, free, and gets those "happy hormones" (called endorphins) rushing around your body. Build up from ten minutes until you can do thirty minutes. If you can do that three days a week, you will see real progress in how you feel.

What people say...
"I can't believe how just going out for a brisk walk each day has changed me. I thought I was far too tired to walk even slowly! But oddly, after walking I feel less tired and full of energy. And my mood is so much better. Thank God."
Ben

Things we need to know about depression

Eating more healthily can lift our mood, and, apparently, rewarding ourselves by doing something we enjoy can boost our immune system and get those happy hormones giving us a lift.

Let's get out of here

1. "Grabbing the moment" is one of the crucial aspects of taking our first steps away from depression. *Grab that positive thought and do it!* The more you practise it, the better you get at it.

2. Don't beat yourself up by thinking you're not doing it well enough. If you push yourself too much, you might end up sinking back into bed and deciding that being a slob is better.

3. Easier than exercise, but just as good at getting the happy hormones dashing around our body, helping our

mood to lift, is to laugh. My favourite ways to get myself laughing when I feel really low are: Bill Bryson books, those clips of films on the web of cats doing the most extraordinary things, those silly television programmes with home videos of birthday parties ending up in mayhem. I really do feel great after laughing.

4. Psychologists say that even smiling can help to reduce stress hormones, so smile at everyone you meet today.

5. If it's pouring with rain and a walk doesn't seem a good idea, put on some music and dance. No one is watching you, so let rip and pretend that you're at the best rock concert ever. Shout. Scream. Let it all out.

6. Put on something like Tchaikovsky's *1812 Overture* and imagine yourself as the drummer – and being in charge of the cannons! Psychologists say that if you enjoy yourself and play like a child, it lifts a low mood.

Building self-esteem

1. Making healthy choices is the start of wanting good things for ourselves.

2. Almost certainly underneath your depression low self-esteem is lurking. As you work through this book, try to be aware of how you put yourself down, and focus on the self-esteem points at the end of each chapter.

3. You will take a big step out of depression if you congratulate yourself about what you did today – for example, reading this chapter!

✔ It's OK

If you don't feel able to do much, make your first step treating yourself gently. Absolutely no beating yourself up allowed!

2

Hiding behind "I'm fine" vs. Acknowledging the truth

The new and difficult feelings we can get with depression can be so weird and uncomfortable that it's only natural we want to retreat and hide.

- What on earth's happening to me?
- Surely someone would have told me that life could get like this.
- The only way through this is to tell everyone that I'm fine.
- I must just keep going – not give in. Everyone relies on me.
- I don't understand why the world has gone very silent.
- I feel I can't communicate with anyone.

There is a whole collection of things we can blame for not being our usual bouncy selves.

- It's my hormones/thyroid/post flu/hay fever.
- I've not been the same since I was made redundant/Dad died.
- The divorce really got to me/I'm missing my pet dog who died/I'm fat, forty and single.
- I've been working eighty-hour weeks, so I'm just tired.

The truth is that all of the above "excuses" can be part of the reason we are depressed. Any big life event, even ones we really want such as a change of house, a new baby, promotion, can all lead us to feel we have lost something special. These new things, although truly wanted, can lead to so much stress that we sink under the strain.

And things that some might regard as "minor" can upset us so much that we feel embarrassed.

What people say...
"I longed for this baby for almost fifteen years. We had all kinds of medical help and when they put him in my arms I knew I should be happy, but I burst into tears. I still feel utterly miserable and I know I'm being a hopeless mother. Everyone keeps telling me to pull myself together for the baby's sake. I do try to be better but I'd rather just lie down and die."
Janice, aged 36

Recognize the truth
When Janice was talking to me I pointed out to her that she's being truthful to herself. She acknowledges that she's miserable and feels worthless, and that's a great starting point.

In fact acknowledging the truth is the very best starting

point from which to take those first tentative steps out of depression.

Things we need to know about depression

It can be common:
- to have physical pain that doesn't have a clear cause;
- to feel the world is against us (paranoia);
- to have obsessive thoughts, possibly in an extreme case leading to OCD (Obsessive Compulsive Disorder);
- to be afraid of crowds, going out of the house or feeling a whole range of things we don't understand;
- to experience nightmares, weird thoughts or have hallucinations – and to find ourselves behaving oddly.

No, you're not going mad! This is your body asking you to listen to it and get some help.

What people say...
"I want to be at the top of my career before I'm thirty, so there's no way I'm giving in to this. I must keep going."
   Philip, aged 27

Denial
Telling ourselves we are "fine" when we aren't is part of what mental health professionals call "denial". The more we stick with "I'm fine" the more we will stay trapped with our feet firmly sucked into the slough of despond.
   Yes, the truth hurts, but it also sets us free. (Eventually!)

Mythbuster

If I just keep these feelings deeply buried inside me they will eventually go away and I'll be able to cope.

If we repress our feelings they tend to jump out at us when we're least expecting them. So it's a better long-term plan to try to let our feelings out gradually, ideally talking them through with someone. But it's OK to "wear a mask" in order to get through the day.

Times when we need to say "I'm fine"

Of course, if someone says to us, "How are you?" it's likely that they don't really want to hear what we're truly feeling! That's just how some cultures work. If we say, "Well, to be honest I'm feeling suicidal," people will run away from us, never to come near us again. (With some people, of course, that might not be a bad thing!)

We need to practise "wearing a mask" to hide what we really feel in order to cope with life. And we also need to learn to say something neutral that is culturally acceptable, such as:

- "Doing OK, thanks."
- "Struggling on."
- "One day at a time."

That last one is particularly useful because it contains a great truth of surviving depression – one small step at a time. But don't fall back into denial!

What people say...

"I remember the day I just walked into the doctor's surgery and said I wanted to see her today. The receptionist smiled at me and told me to sit down and wait till the doctor was free. I

sat there, flipping through the magazines, feeling terrified but strangely peaceful. Talking to the doctor was really hard. I felt so stupid. But that day was my first step out of the dark pit I'd been in for months."

Linda

Who am I?

A great many people who become depressed say that they don't really know themselves very well, and that was certainly true for me in my earlier life. (I'm still working on it!)

If we don't know ourselves, we're likely not to have a clue why the Big D has struck. That is seriously bad news.

It probably sounds a bit scary to find out more about who we are. But we need to remember that the place we're in – the slough of despond – is so dire that taking some steps to get out is a good idea, no matter how painful it might be.

Things we need to know about depression

Depression is often about some kind of loss, so if you can find a quiet space and jot down some of your losses, you'll almost certainly get some insight into what's happening in your inner life.

- Did someone put you down when you were a child, causing you to feel "no good"? This kind of damage to our self-esteem can take a lifetime to repair. (That is why there are self-esteem points at the end of each chapter. You *can* change how you see yourself.)
- Does someone now rob you of your sense of being an OK person?
- Have you lost something significant recently? Your good health? Are your children leaving home? Or

have you lost your home itself or a special belonging in a mugging or perhaps the ability to have children?
- Have you had a significant birthday that makes you feel you're "past it"?

Losses come back to haunt us

If we lost someone dear to us when we were young, that sense of abandonment can be reawakened when someone we love dies or leaves us.

The sense that we were not loved unconditionally can be so damaging to our self-esteem that it can affect our own ability to love unconditionally. From talking to other mothers I can see that the fear I had as a young mother – that I wouldn't be able to love my children enough – is very common.

We worry we will be hopeless parents because we are depressed – and all that negative thinking just sends us further down into the mire.

These are huge steps!

Yes, OK, the things I've listed above are life-changing, life-shattering and the journey away from them can be lifelong. But if we are to get better from depression, it does mean looking hard at those inner losses of love and attachment.

If you just take one of the losses you've identified, you can work on that – and just that, for a while. (Take the journey slowly and gently.)

You might want to jot down some thoughts such as:

- What my uncle did to me deeply affected my ability to trust people.
- I never felt I belonged in my family.
- I hated being teased.
- I was bullied at school and that was the biggest event in my childhood.
- When my wife left me I felt my life had stopped.
- My parents don't even try to understand me.
- I'm desperate not to be single.

What makes me "me"?

There is more to understanding "who we are" than working out our losses, but that is one good place to start.

I found writing a journal of my thoughts helped me enormously to work out what was going on in my inner world. Once I'd written something down, it was easier to think about it – and to work out what I was doing to keep myself stuck in the bog.

I worked out that:

- I can't cope with any kind of conflict.
- I take even minor criticism as total devastation and proof that the world would be a better place if I was dead.
- I believed my mother when she said I was a hopeless and useless person who would "never come to anything".

It took me many years to work through these things – but I worked out what was going on in my head and that helped me to get beyond these irrational beliefs and insecurities.

Knowing ourselves a bit better is going to help us to take those first steps away from the Big D.

What people say...
"I absolutely loathe myself."
  Asif

Drugs and alcohol will help to get me through this phase.
No! Alcohol lowers your mood, sometimes in a spectacular way, and drugs mess with your mind. It's hard enough as it is to cling onto reality in depression, so don't make it even worse.

I'm better off than...
Some people try to shake us out of depression by telling us about those worse off than us – starving people in Africa and so on. Yes, at one level that can be true. But it's another one of those thoughts that can keep us trapped in denial. Of course it would be horrendous to be living through a famine, but our own pain of getting through depression is just as real – and it's *our* pain. We must deal with it.

Let's get out of here
One way to take our first steps out of depression is to try to access our real feelings. That can be really scary, but try to write a list of feelings you've had over the last few weeks. Here are some suggestions:
- frustration
- insecurity

- sadness
- annoyance
- exhaustion
- shame
- guilt
- fear.

More about feelings in the next chapter.

Building self-esteem

1. You *are* an OK valuable person. All your negative "self-talk" (I'm hopeless, etc.) was put in your head by parents, teachers, and others. What you lost was your sense that you are OK. That's a huge loss to have to deal with. But if you go on taking small steps away from depression, your "OK-ness" can come back.

2. If you are realistic and admit that you need help, that doesn't mean that you are a "weak" person. It means you are an honest person who is getting in touch with some scary feelings.

3. Accept mishaps as part of normal life.

✔ It's OK

It's OK if all you can do today is think of just one of your feelings. When you are ready to think further about all of this, your inner spirit – the core of who you are as a person, the bit of you that responds in love and smiles when you see a puppy – will bring things to your attention.

All of this awfulness *will* come to an end.

3

Drowning in worries vs. Developing strategies to reduce stress

It's very common to experience huge anxiety alongside depression. That doesn't make the depression any less valid. For years I thought that in some strange way my depression wasn't "real" and I was being neurotic and pathetic, after one psychiatrist said to me, with a considerable amount of derision in his voice, "You're just anxious, not depressed."

They go together
Anxiety and depression seem to go together in some people like chocolate brownies and vanilla ice cream, but it's not easy to unravel what is making us panic. Just making a start on one small thing is all we need in order to understand our anxiety better.

- Why was I so upset when she said that?
- Why did I do that? That's not my usual response to that kind of thing.

Eventually I worked out that I spent all my waking hours feeling as if I was walking along the edge of a precipice. One false move and I'd be annihilated.

It has taken me many years to get rid of that debilitating feeling to the point where I understood *why* I felt that anxious.

Touching our core

Depression can cause us to look inwards to the centre of our being. Although some people think this is a bad thing, actually it's crucial to our journey.

Many people, especially if they are older and were brought up to put on a brave face, push difficult feelings down inside themselves, denying their existence. They only want to hear us say, "I'm fine." (See Chapter 2.)

What people say...
"Repression is deadly."
Nella Last in her diary, *Nella Last's War*

In order to get out of depression, we need to understand at least something about what those real feelings are.

Yes, this can be seriously scary – and, yes, it will to some extent make things feel a bit worse for a while. But only in the same sense that getting a raging toothache sorted means you have to get through the pain of the dentist. In the end, the awful pain we have to go through leads to a better life in the long term.

If I worry about something for long enough, the worry will go away.
Spending lots of time worrying actually makes us more worried. Try allowing yourself ten minutes to fret about something, then tell yourself firmly that you are now going to shut it out of your mind and get on with more positive things.

What are my deepest feelings?

If you're like me, even naming some of your feelings is terribly hard. I think this could be because we've had so much happening to us that is awful, so we switch off our feelings in order to survive. We become a bit numb. So here is a list of ways you might be feeling that I hope will help you to identify what's going on deep inside you.

- remote
- passive
- pessimistic
- hostile
- envious
- irritable
- distraught
- self-conscious
- thankful
- empowered
- upset
- guilty
- bewildered
- disgusted

Drowning in worries vs. Developing strategies to reduce stress **31**

- insecure
- lonely
- ashamed
- shy
- sorry
- restless
- contemptuous
- apathetic
- discouraged
- curious
- free
- amazed
- hopeful
- bereaved
- heartbroken
- forlorn
- nostalgic
- vulnerable
- afraid.

Understanding our deepest feelings?

Your feelings might well be a tangle of pain that is very hard to sort out. I worked out eventually that I was devastated by the death of my grandfather when I was five. It had left in me a powerful sense of having been abandoned. And this grew into such a huge fear of being abandoned again that it was spoiling loving relationships I was in.

It took me years to work that out, so we're not talking

here of things you can necessarily figure out this week – but every journey begins with a single step.

Things we can't change
We're back again to our remarkable tendency to be trying to change things that cannot be changed.

This is toe-curlingly daft and a huge drain on our nervous energy – and the patience of those around us. Things like:

- I'm ninety-three, and that's awful.
- My partner has died.
- My child has emigrated.
- I've got MS.

Moaning and worrying about anything that cannot be changed is a habit we need to break. We *can* change what we are thinking about. For example, we can learn to stop ourselves thinking the very worst of everything.

The deathbed test
I think it's quite usual to worry about everything when we're depressed, from the muddy footprints we left in the kitchen when we came in from the garden, to the cat being missing for three days. I really was a phenomenally good worrier until a lovely psychologist taught me how to apply the "deathbed test".

I learned to distinguish the small worries from the big ones. The muddy footprints are easily sorted, but the missing cat is a big one.

But neither of them is a worry that we'll think about on our deathbed, so why worry about them now? As I've learned to use the deathbed test I've noticed that worries that I definitely labelled as deathbed ones in the past now aren't. I've moved on. Those old desperate worries have faded a little.

Worst case scenario

My lovely friend Lynne told me about her way to combat our fears and anxiety about the future. She asks herself about her worst case scenario.

What people say...

"I tell myself, 'OK, if he dies, of course I'll be devastated.' Then I work through some of the things I'd have to do, and what others would do and say. That's my worst case scenario. The very worst thing in the whole world that could happen to me. And now I know I'd survive it. So I'll be able to cope with other things as well. Just!"
    Lynne

"Worry is like a rocking chair. It gives you something to do, but doesn't get you anywhere!"
    Sally

Things we need to know about depression

Feeling more in control of our worrying can boost our confidence.

My strategies to reduce stress

Sometimes that overwhelming sense of being so tense and worried we can't cope with anything can be made better with some fairly simple stress-busting techniques.

- If I lie down, tense every muscle in my body a few times, then let go of that tension one part of my body at a time, I feel less stressed.

- If I put on music and either dance to it or sit or lie

down and relax, I get rid of that feeling that a herd of elephants is stampeding through my body.

- If I go out and do some vigorous exercise, my world feels much safer and my level of anxiety is reduced.

- If I watch television or a favourite film, this takes me into another world and my heart stops pounding. (Yes, it is escapism, but sometimes that's exactly what is needed to allow our inner spirit to soar. It isn't repression.)

- If I do something enjoyable, such as taking my little dog to the park, it makes me smile to see her delight at chasing squirrels, and the exercise gets those happy hormones going.

- If I meditate on something beautiful and nurture my spirituality, that quiet inner space gives me a few moments of connecting with the peace and joy of the universe.

What people say...
"Spiritual beliefs give us a context larger than ourselves, which can provide us with perspective. It needn't be formal worship but more of a reflective time in your day to contemplate something you believe in."
A psychologist

Let's get out of here

1. Can you write the word for your deepest feeling? If it feels like an impenetrable mess then draw that mess! Go on. Just scribble it.

2. Can you work on finding ways to relax your body? Lavender oil and gently massaging your body can help.

3. Psychologists say that if our world feels chaotic, that can increase our anxiety, and if we create some rituals

in our life, that can reduce stress, partly because we save time and partly because rituals can be comforting. So, for example, if we always deal with our paperwork (emails, bills, etc.) with a cup of tea immediately after breakfast, this can stop them building up to an unmanageable pile of things to do.

Building self-esteem

1. It might take you a long time to work out the reasons for your anxiety, but if you can start to make a real list (not just a list in your head) that's a great start. Is it family? Love or lack of it? Anger? Feeling unable to forgive someone?

2. Then do the deathbed test on these worries.

3. Learning to worry only about things that deserve to be worried about is a fundamental rule of life. Can you identify any really daft things you worry about? Can you create a list of things that you are going to stop worrying about because:

   a) you can't change these things (and that includes people)

   b) they are so small they don't deserve to be taking up so much of your thinking time?

4. Perhaps you'll be able to say something like, "Wow! Instead of spending an hour worrying about that, I wrote a poem and cleaned the bath instead. How about that for some positive, practical action! Well done, me."

✔ It's OK

We might have learned to be a worrier from birth, so it's likely to take time and energy to walk away from it all. It's OK just to take one small step today. But come back to this chapter and work through it again, because allowing yourselves to go on worrying is likely to ruin your life!

4

Doing what others want vs. Making our own decisions

Sometimes we can have so little trust in ourselves that we:

- do and say what we think others want us to do and say;
- copy others' beliefs and ways of life in the hope this will make us acceptable and keep our fear of being rejected at bay;
- live our life according to the expectations that others have of us;
- respond to questions such as "What shall we do this afternoon?" with, "I don't mind. I'll do what you want to do."

Of course, so much of life has to revolve around our depression that doing what others want is probably sometimes a good idea. But if we repeatedly refuse to make at least some attempt to make decisions for ourselves (however difficult), we are in some ways not being who we truly are.

What people say...
"I knew I was letting my mother down. All my life I've tried to please her. But I'm not the daughter she hoped for."
   Katie, 23-year-old student

Being "ourselves"
We need to try to detect in those around us what their unrealistic expectations of us are. This is particularly true when we are children – including adult "children". We might have spent our whole life trying to do what our parents wanted, and the bit of us that is truly "ourselves" – our inner spirit, our soul, the central point of who we are – could be getting squashed. That is no way to travel through life because we can become:

- stressed, frustrated, and exhausted;
- deeply angry – even if we can't show that anger and are completely unaware that it is there within us.

Finding "ourselves" can be a long and difficult search, but one way to help our search is to ask ourselves:

What kind of person do I really want to be?

The big question
This question appears several times in this book because it is something we must ask ourselves if we are to get out of depression. I think of this question as us learning to shine a light into the core of who we are. To answer this question you might find it helpful to think ahead:

- Where do I want to be in five years' time?
- Do I want to be a grumpy miserable person who just sees the negative aspect of everything?
- What's my aim in life?

In the depths of depression these questions are likely to seem meaningless. We may well have absolutely no idea where we want to get to – and even if we did, we probably wouldn't have the energy to get there anyway.

But as we begin to recover, it can be crucial to think through where we want our journey through life to take us.

What can I control?

Of course, we don't have control over some aspects of our life. If our depression is partly triggered by long-term illness, or because we are elderly and unable to live an independent life, all we can do is learn to accept these difficult things.

But we do have control over much of our everyday decision-making.

What people say...
"What did you do today to make your life better?"
   A character in the film *American History X*

When I first heard this said in the film, my immediate reaction was that wanting to make your own life better is selfish and instead it's better to try to make the lives of others better. But I realized that this is an "oxygen mask" issue.

On the first transatlantic flight I did with my family, I listened to the instruction in the safety demo to put my own oxygen mask on first in an emergency, then help my children. I thought this was the wrong way round. I *must* help my children first.

But no. If I'm not OK, I can't help my children. It's one of those rare occasions when "me first" is best. (Usually "me first" is what ruins relationships.)

We *can* control:

- what we do today;
- decisions we take in order to make our life better;
- what myths about depression we are telling ourselves.

We might say: "Whenever I'm rejected or treated unfairly I must interpret this as a catastrophe and those people must be damned."
This can be how we think, so trying to teach ourselves to be more balanced can reduce our stress.

Trying to be "Super-person"

One way to make our life better is to try to shed some light on why we behave in certain ways. For example, if we had parents who expected too much of us, we might be left with an overwhelming drive to be "Super-person".

This isn't an aspect of depression for everyone, of course. But some of us become depressed because we are trying too hard – and, of course, we crack up.

It might be that:

- we have lost our perspective of what is important in life;
- we feel the need to drive ourselves, maybe to prove something and make up for something we lost long ago;
- we feel we need to work hard to deserve to be loved;
- we are trying to win approval by doing more and more and more.

Working too hard?

Rushing around working hard isn't wrong. We'd never get through school or complete an artistic endeavour or bring up children well without slogging hour after hour on the things we need or want to do.

Hard work doesn't inevitably lead to depression. But tiredness – such an ordinary part of life – can be a trigger for a downward spiralling of our mood.

I'm indispensable

The truth is that none of us are indispensable. Even a breastfeeding mother can be replaced sometimes by a kind person with a bottle of milk with no harm whatsoever to Baby.

We need to accept that the world will not fall apart if we take a break or take some days off work or get a babysitter. Yes, it might take some planning. But if it means you spend less time in that dark slough of despond, isn't it worth it?

Setting realistic goals

I'm one of those people who think that when I'm feeling positive, I can take on the world. I get "high" – and totally unrealistic about what I can do. I plan to make several quilts, write a dozen more books, take on all kinds of teaching – and generally stack up so much in my diary that when reality strikes, I'm devastated at all my commitments.

This is exhausting and daunting. But it's all much better than it used to be because at least I know that I do it, and am learning to curb my enthusiasm to take on the world.

Things we need to know about depression

If you are having extreme mood swings with "highs" that feel a bit out of control, it's crucial you tell your doctor. (Your "highs" might mean, for example, you spend too much money or you expect far too much of yourself.)

Knowing ourselves

We're back again to the fact that knowing ourselves is crucial to our journey out of depression. I think it's like having an inner "map" of who we are. I taught myself to remember that I take on too much and I "look" with my inner light at what I've learned about myself and make myself be sensible. (That was really hard at first!)

One aspect of my "map" is the list in my head of all the things I'm *never* going to do – *ever*.

So in my daily work, instead of going around the house and garden saying, "I must do that" and, "That needs sorting," I just give things away (such as old sleeping bags that I've spent thirty years telling myself I'm going to transform into quilts). I tell myself, "That's on my list of things I'm never going to do."

That way I've got rid of the nagging sense that there are a thousand things waiting for me to do.

Making lists

Writing lists can bring some sense of order to our lives. We can see these as a "map" to get us through today. But I learned long ago that I tend to make mine stupidly long and completely unrealistic!

One of my Depression Alliance friends, Paul, said that at the top of our list we need to write "breathe in and out". We can then tick that and feel that we are getting on with our day. When we do the next small task, we can check that off, and so on. That way we get a sense of success and that makes us feel good.

And even a split second of a glimpse of happiness is an inner light that shines on our "map", showing us the way out of depression.

Let's get out of here

1. Consider how you might find out more about yourself so that you can make more of your own decisions about your life.

   - Writing poems or painting pictures can help us to develop your "inner light".

   - Seek out groups that you might be able to join (see the Useful Resources section at the end of this book).

   - Start that mental list of things that you are never going to do – ever.

2. "What did I do today to make my life better?" You could write this question on a sticky note and put it somewhere you will read it each day.

Building self-esteem

1. You don't need to be "Super-person" to be a good and loving person. You just need to be a good-enough parent, a good-enough employee, a good-enough artist, and so on. You're a valuable person, just as you are. (You could write that on a sticky note as well and stick it where you will see it every day.)

2. It's OK to say "no" to people, including your children, partner, parents, boss, and needy neighbour.

In the depths of depression life can feel so confusing that even writing a list of things to do feels too hard. But if you can write a little about your feelings, this has been shown to relieve emotional stress – even something as simple as "Today I feel sad" would be a great start.

5

Wandering without a map vs. Creating boundaries

Being depressed can tend to make us feel that we are just stumbling randomly through life, with no idea where we're going and no idea how to make our lives less chaotic.

If we can work on having some kind of "map" this can help us reduce our levels of stress. Developing rituals like these might be helpful:

- Washing the dishes every evening so we don't start the next day feeling that life has defeated us already.

- Always keeping our keys in exactly the same place so we don't lose them and have to go through the stress of frantic searches.

- Always having a day off or at least some time that is just for us to rest, meditate, do something creative to feed our inner spirit, and be unburdened of any kind of responsibility.

What do I prefer?
Creating these rituals can diminish our sense that life is unpredictably stressful. It helps us to have the emotional energy to get on with that crucial quest – to find out more about our True Self.

Although we are all unique (and isn't that absolutely mind-bogglingly great?), there are some common "types" of people, and exploring those can shed some light on who we are and what our preferences are. For example:

- There are some who find being with people really exhausting.
- Others absolutely live for the times they can go out with their friends.
- Some people are vague and dreamy and aren't very good at being realistic or finishing a task.
- Others are much more focused and good at completing what they set out to do.
- Some people have ten good ideas before coffee time, but need help to know which of their ideas are feasible.
- Others find any kind of creative thinking more difficult and prefer to be given instructions so they know what to do.

None of what's in the above list is "wrong". Some people are just born and brought up to behave differently. We just are "that type of person", with preferences about our lifestyle.

Who have I become?
But some aspects of our personality are much more about

who we have become through the things that life has thrown at us.

- Some of us behave like doormats and let others walk all over us.

- Some are such perfectionists that they are never satisfied. Goals are always unreachable so they can be frustrated and disappointed.

- Some people are so self-absorbed that they fail to see the effects they have on people around them.

We can all be a bit selfish, especially when we are depressed. In a sense, we need to focus on our own needs to journey out of depression. But overdoing it can cause problems for those around us.

Also, I have seen some people recover from depression, but stay self-absorbed. They haven't developed enough self-awareness to realize that they can be difficult to live with, selfish, and thoroughly annoying!

Difficult people

You have probably worked out that some people are harder to be with than others, but sometimes our lives mean we can be intimately involved with those we find difficult.

It's terribly hard to be real and genuine because obviously it makes us vulnerable when we show people who we really are (and this is another aspect of life that can make us so very afraid). When we find someone difficult it's even harder to allow them to see who we really are because we may know from experience that they cannot be trusted with personal information about us.

Making healthier relationships

It is crucial for us to find out who we really are – what is our True Self. This knowledge is going to be an essential part of our "map" to find our way out of depression.

Our depression can be the result of being stuck in a "toxic" relationship, whether it's with our partner, boss, friend or a family member. If someone is difficult, it could well be that we need to make our boundaries clearer in order to find – and protect – our true self. (Remember that we can't usually change other people!)

Signs that we need to work on our boundaries include:

- our sense of shame;
- finding it hard to say "no";
- getting involved with people who end up being bad for us;
- being over-sensitive to criticism;
- taking onto ourselves too much of what another person is feeling, and feeling burdened by the responsibility;
- having difficulty asking for what we need;
- feeling that our happiness depends on other people;
- not giving ourselves time for creative activities we enjoy;
- struggling to know what we really feel.

If you feel that any of those are part of your life, it's likely that you need to make or strengthen some of your boundaries so that others don't:

- smother your attempts to be "real";
- invade your space (physical, emotional or spiritual);
- attack your hopes and dreams;
- intrude into your thoughts, taking over your inner sense of peace.

The only way to find love is to be a "doormat" and give up my own peace of mind.

This can be a hard one to struggle out of, but it's important to be true to ourselves and to learn to be a bit more assertive.

Another "oxygen mask" moment

If one or more people are invading our personal space, it might mean that we are spending inappropriate amounts of time trying to please them or attending to their needs *at the expense of our own.*

This is another one of those rare instances where "me first" is important. (Mostly "me first" is what ruins our life.) For example, I'm quite sure that my mother saw me as an extension of herself. But she was probably completely unaware of that, as I was until I was in my forties. Once I realized the extent of her manipulation of me, it enabled me to make some much more effective boundaries. I realized, for example, that I didn't need to dress the way she wanted me to or drink my tea with no milk but with lemon instead, as she did.

I could instead be "me", and this enabled me to find my True Self, and that helped me to be a better mother and partner because my relationship with my mother was healthier.

It also helped me realize that I was able to take steps away from long-term influences on my life that were keeping me repeatedly depressed. And when I began to realize that I was able to change some of these long-term influences, it gave a huge boost to my sense of being an OK person.

Creating boundaries and order in our lives

If we can make some decisions that will make our lives better, like those I made about my mother, this can help us to have *more order in our lives*, and therefore more peace and contentment. We'll have a "map" to help us to find the right pathway to a much better quality of life.

What people say...

"Submitting to others, rather than affirming our own reality... we give up our own inner world in order to be accepted by others... We give up ourselves in order to please, satisfy or impress others. By betraying our True Self, our sense of integrity and wholeness suffers. Our spirit wilts."
John Amodeo

Things we need to know about depression

Psychologists say that if we seek the company of optimistic people with high self-esteem – people we admire – their positive attitude rubs off on us.

Finding the right "map"

As well as finding a "map" to help us towards knowing who we truly are, we also need to decide where we want to get to once we've taken a few steps along the way.

The pilgrim in John Bunyan's book, *Pilgrim's Progress*, was trying to find the "right" path for a life of goodness and keeping away from anything that was "evil". We make decisions many times during a day that affect the path we are choosing to take – how we treat the delivery person who interrupts our day, and our attitude to the person at the checkout in the shop.

So if we want to find contentment in our lives, we

need to come back to that big question about the kind of person we want to be.

What kind of person do we want to be?
There are some things we can't choose about our lives (such as who our mother is!) – but we can choose:

• how we behave;

• how we treat others;

• what our goals in life are

– and although it's hard, we can choose how we think (more of that in Chapter 9).

If we are thinking, "I'll get revenge one day," or something equally negative, we are likely to stay depressed and not be following a particularly helpful "map".

But if we set out to make our life as good as it can be, and do the best we can for those around us, this will lead us to a greater sense of peace – and to that elusive sense of joy we so long for.

Facts about depression
Gaining more self-understanding about how we think and feel can help us recover.

Let's get out of here
If you need more help with sorting out your personal boundaries, you might want to talk to a trusted friend about it or find a book in the library that will help. I've found Charles Whitfield's book *Boundaries and Relationships* very helpful (see Useful Resources at the end of the book).

Building self-esteem

1. Try to spend time with people who have a positive outlook on life. People we admire who are optimistic and have high self-esteem can contribute to our own growing sense of self-esteem.

2. Being around "losers" or those who manipulate or who are self-centred could be pulling us back into the mire.

3. You might think of self-help groups as being gloomy, but all the ones I've been to are full of kind and generous people who don't sit around moaning. They can be places where we can be honest about our feelings, but also upbeat. Being with others who are struggling can be a source of healing.

✔ It's OK

If just about every aspect of needing to create healthier boundaries in this chapter applies to you, join the club!

Apparently even really sensibly balanced people need to make some relationships healthier. So plod on. One step at a time.

6

Drowning in negative thinking vs. Choosing to think more positively

Do you know what your inner world is saying to you? If you don't know what I mean, it could be that you aren't aware of or listening to your "negative self-talk".

What people say...
"I know I should be able to manage my life better. I ought to be able to be on top of my job and not let things get so chaotic. Lots of people are helping me, but I suppose I'm just not a good enough person. I'm really feeble and that's hard for a bloke like me to admit."
Tariq

We can be completely unaware of what we are saying to ourselves – and not realize that these thoughts we throw at ourselves are keeping us depressed.

- I'm not good enough.
- I always have bad luck.
- Whatever I do goes wrong.

I realized that I was saying negative things like that and they were a vital part of what I believed about myself and the world around me. I *interpreted* the world in a negative way.

- I was jumping to negative conclusions. If someone was late meeting me, I thought they weren't coming – and why would they want to meet someone as hopeless as me anyway?

- I didn't allow other interpretations. For example, if someone didn't respond to my message, I didn't let myself consider that they might not have got it. I assumed instead that they were rejecting me.

- I made completely over-the-top generalizations. If something went wrong, such as an issue with my children, I'd immediately say, "I'm a totally hopeless mother."

- I assumed all the responsibility if something went wrong, even if I wasn't responsible for the event.

- If I made a mistake, my whole world exploded.

- If anyone criticized anything to do with me, I immediately took this as profound criticism of who I was – and I'd feel it so personally that I could get suicidal.

You will be able to see that I was in a complete mess:
- I felt guilty all the time.
- I was turning life into a series of catastrophes.
- I was taking responsibility for things that were not my problem.

- And I was thinking about these "bad" things over and over and over again!

Wow! Writing these lists has been challenging. I keep telling myself what a stupid idiot I was. So clearly I'm not through my negative thinking yet. But I know I've made many steps away from where I was and that process for me involved:

- talking and writing thousands of words;
- therapy;
- allowing myself to be loved and accepted.

Our irrational beliefs

As I worked through that process of teaching myself to challenge my negative thinking, I discovered that I held a great many completely irrational beliefs (this is where the "Mythbusters" come from):

- If someone doesn't smile at me, it is evidence that they hate me, just like everyone else.
- Unless I get one hundred per cent approval from everyone around me, it shows that I deserve to be dead.
- I must be totally competent and achieve brilliantly at everything.

No wonder I was depressed!

Mythbuster

I cannot control or change my feelings, because they are controlled by others.
This is a very common belief in depressed people – and it's not true! We usually have much more control over our own feelings than we think we do.

Changing how we think

We *can* change how we think. But we need to go gently with it while we are very depressed. For example, can you stop reading and jot down just one negative thought you've had in the last few minutes? What about:

- Well, it might be easy for Sue to change, but I'm far too hopeless to be able to do it.

- I don't think I can do this. It sounds too hard.

We must challenge those negative thoughts, otherwise they can take over our lives and it is this negativity, psychologists say, that is holding us in the lethargy of depression.

- If your thought is that it all sounds too hard for you, can you counteract that with something more rational? "Well, others have managed to change their negative thinking, so as long as I give myself time, I can do it too. I'll write down just one negative thought a day and work on it."

- If you said to yourself, "I don't know where to start – I'm too overwhelmed," can you challenge that? "I'll start, right now. I really want to get out of depression."

How do I recognize negative thinking?

Our "shoulds" and "oughts" are fairly easy to spot. "I should have known better" and "I ought to have done that differently" can be challenged with something like this:

- Everyone can be wise after the event. But no one has the benefit of hindsight beforehand, including me.

- I'm human and make mistakes, but probably I won't worry about this on my deathbed, so I'm not going to let myself worry about it now.

Another thing about "shoulds" and "oughts" is that they are often about rules we've made up for ourselves. Think about that one. Can you identify these rules you have?

- "I should have been able to be a better mother." This is a big one for me, and I learned to say that I was a "good enough" mother.

- "I ought to be able to keep my mother happy" was one of mine, and many times I've heard depressed people trying to take responsibility for the happiness of others.

Of course it's great to be able to contribute to the happiness of those we love. But watch out you haven't made a rule for yourself that is impossible to abide by.

Listening to our thinking

It was only as I talked to people that I became aware of my negative thinking. You could share this chapter with someone you trust, and ask them to talk about it with you.

Another way to "listen" to what we are thinking is to use writing to become more self-aware.

- A few jottings about our day can be powerful, especially if we try to log our sense of enjoyment. For example, I dread going out of the house or having to phone someone. I put it off because I think I will hate doing it. The sense of not wanting to do the things is awful, so I write that down. Then after I've been out or phoned the person, I log how I actually feel about it. Almost inevitably I experienced a sense of satisfaction – even pleasure.

- We can look at our list of things for the day and decide to give each one some stars according to the level of enjoyment we think we will have as we do it. So cooking dinner we might give only one star. "I hate doing it." "It takes so long. I'm such a hopeless cook anyway." But afterwards, what are our feelings now? How many stars of enjoyment? Again, almost inevitably we feel more positive about it than we thought we would.

And that is the key thought in this chapter.

- Probably we have more pleasure throughout our day than we think we have.

- It's our negative thinking that is keeping us depressed.

- We probably do more than we think we do. (Remember, top of your list is breathe in and out. You did that, so move on to the next thing.)

- Things that we dread and avoid are usually less awful than we think.

Mythbuster

The way to deal with things that upset me is to think about them all day, and still be thinking about them next week, month... year.
Worrying about something for ten minutes is more than enough! If we give too much time and energy to worrying about the past or the future, we risk not having enough mental energy for today.

Are you a ruminator?
If you are a world champion ruminator like I am, you are letting the same negative thoughts go around and around and around in your brain.

Apparently more women than men are ruminators, and it's almost certainly seriously affecting your journey away from depression.

But if you work at monitoring your thinking, you'll be able to identify if you're letting yourself focus on something too much.

Things we need to know about depression

Thinking negatively traps us in depression, anxiety, and low self-esteem.

Don't take on the world
Just as we need to check that we haven't got unrealistic lists of things to do today, so it's important not to try to change how we think in one month. If we scrutinize everything we are doing and obsessively write it all down, we will just end up collapsing in exhaustion.

Positive thinking
Having worked out at least one of our negative ways of interpreting our world, we need to learn to transform that thinking into something that will enable us to get back on the road to healing. For example:

- I keep a work diary of the number of hours I sit at my desk. It helps me to focus and not to say at the end of a day, "I've hardly done anything today. I'm hopeless." Instead I say, "OK, only three hours today, but I went swimming and did some shopping."

- I worked out that I was a world expert at "catastrophizing"! I could turn any minor incident into the end of my existence. But I learned to apply the deathbed test: if I won't worry about this on my deathbed, why am I worrying about it now?

Let's get out of here

1. One of the early ways I began to access my negative thoughts was to count them and keep a tally on a bit of paper. A psychologist suggested I do this and the outcome was terrifying. I was thinking negatively nearly all the time!

2. You could just pick one aspect of your negative thinking and work out how to make it more positive, perhaps by talking to someone or spotting your "shoulds".

3. See the Useful resources section at the end for books on changing negative thinking.

Building self-esteem

If we do something wrong, it doesn't prove that we are a bad person. It just shows that we are a fallible human being who sometimes behaves badly or misjudges a situation.

✔ It's OK

If you discover that most of your thinking is negative, remember that this is "the depression talking" and it will get better as you challenge it. Then your thoughts will change – and so will your inner being.

7

Blaming others vs. Taking responsibility for ourselves

It's an essential aspect of taking steps out of depression to grasp that:

- life isn't fair, and
- bad things happen to good people.

These are aspects of life on planet earth that we cannot change – however much we worry about them and grind our teeth in rage.

It's your fault!

"It's your fault. You started it!" were words that I heard most days as a primary school teacher. Probably seven-year-olds have to work through blaming others when things go wrong, but it's very worrying when people in mid-life are still saying, "It's her fault," and allowing themselves to be trapped in habits of retaliation.

What people say...
"My doctor is a bit hopeless and she insisted that I work with the community psychiatric nurse, but she's pathetic. I can't get the help I need and they keep telling me to go for some in-depth therapy, but I know that will make everything worse – if it's possible for things to get worse than they are already. I just sit at home all day because I can't work. No one will give me a job. It's my family's fault that I'm like this in the first place. I'm forty-six and I know I'm not going to find love and have children. It's not fair."
Jessica

Yes, it is "their fault"

One of the paradoxes of life is that when we are hurt and treated badly as a child, or in situations where we have no power, it *is* "their fault".

- Jessica (above) had been abused as a child, then rejected by her family when she began to talk about it.

- If a doctor or a colleague or the rogue builder treats us appallingly, yes, it's "their fault" that we are left devastated.

- "Neighbours from hell" might be so noisy and aggressive that life can become intolerable.

- If we are mugged, not only has our money been taken, but also our peace of mind.

All of these things that might be aspects of our fall into the slough of despond are someone else's "fault".

They ruined my life and it's never going to change.

It feels as if this is true, but it's one of the most dangerous negative things we tell ourselves.

He made me angry

The problem with saying, "It's their fault" is that we can lose any sense of power in our lives, and we end up completely stuck in that smelly bog. The only way out is to dump those blaming thoughts. OK, it *was* "their fault", but if you keep that rattling around in your head for long enough, you could go on blaming someone for the rest of your life.If we are to find away to take a first step into a better life, we need to take some responsibility for our feelings.

It took me a long time to work out how to shift my brain from saying, "She made me angry," to, "I became angry when she did that and I know it's OK to be angry, but now I'm going to work through those angry feelings."

I could see it was OK to say, "Depression has made me lethargic," but to stop saying things like, "She made me angry" was really hard. But I had to take responsibility for what I was feeling and thinking. I worked out that my emotions are mine – and I can (with difficulty) control them.

A subtle shift

It's only a tiny shift in emphasis to take responsibility for our feelings instead of blaming someone else, but the effects of making that shift are huge. We can take a step away from depression.

Of course, it can be a long process and when I was trying to make that shift I became very good at blaming

my husband, David, for making me confused and angry!
I still struggle with getting stuck in blaming others, and
I have to force myself to stop both the negative blaming
thoughts and ruminating about past events. I try now to
replace those thoughts with:

- a mental picture of my beautiful grandchildren;
- a smile and thoughts of my lettuces and raspberries
  growing on the allotment;
- a wise thought of Paul the apostle ,who suggests that we
  think about things that are true, and lovely, and pure –
  with our head full of beauty there will be no space for us
  to do negative ruminating.

Blaming isn't lovely. It's hideous stuff that sticks to us and
ruins our lives.

Stuck as a victim
Depression can make us feel:

- powerless;
- totally dependent on others;
- life is out of our control.

These are really horrible feelings and they can push us
further into depression. If we add to that the sense of
apathy we feel, sometimes to the point of wanting to be
dead, this whole blaming thing can keep us recriminating
for decades.

Been there. Done that.

We must find a way out of behaving as a victim if we are
to walk away from depression.

Get back the power
In my book about recovering from abuse I quoted Susan

Jeffers: "Make no mistake. Anytime we blame any one or anything for what is happening in our lives, we are giving away all our power."

A woman wrote to me because she was so angry that I'd included this quote in my book. She said all her problems were her family's fault! But she didn't give me her address, so I couldn't write back to say she'd misunderstood me. Of course it takes time to recover from painful things. Yes, people can be so nasty to each other and it *was* "their fault", but if we keep on believing that, *and keeping it as a major influence on our life,* we are going to:

• be really unhappy;

• stay depressed;

• quite possibly not be a pleasant person to be with.

It's true that depression can make us feel despairing and helpless, but *we must take back the power in our lives*!

If we don't try to take responsibility for our own feelings, and move away from retaliation, we are in danger of letting those people who hurt us have far too much negative influence on our lives for far too long.

Don't let that happen! Turn around!

Let's get out of here

To get back a sense of personal power we can choose to do a range of things that fit with our personal circumstances.

1. Identify who you are blaming for your sadness. What was done to you was awful, and was "their fault".

2. If you've had a tough time and it has deeply affected your life to the point where everything is painful and hideous, *you have to want to change this awful quality of your life if you are going to get out of depression.*

3. Make a commitment to stopping a cycle of blaming

others, rejecting the unhappiness this has led to.

4. Make a promise to yourself today that you will get out of "victim mode" and be determined to get the best life anyone can have rather than ruminating and recriminating.

5. This starts with identifying any "negative thinking" (see also Chapter 6).

6. Then learn to let go by thinking more positively. Try filling your mind with beautiful images, such as peacock butterflies on a buddleia bush or snow on the Yorkshire Dales.

7. Relax. Do some gentle stretches. You're not going to be able to stop blaming others immediately, but you can, today, make a commitment to doing so.

Building self-esteem

If you're saying "I can't do that" to the list of things to do above, that's your low self-esteem ruining your life. That's your low self-esteem keeping you trapped in depression.

Low self-esteem usually arises when one or more people treated you badly. It was "their fault". But if you can see that now you are older you have a bit more power over your life, you can work at building a new life for yourself.

No baby is born thinking "What a hopeless person I am". We get taught that by ruthless and inadequate adults. We can learn to dump the junk by learning how to think more positively.

Things we need to know about depression

Low self-esteem is almost always an underlying cause of depression.

 **✔ It's OK**

If this chapter has resulted in you feeling angry, guilty, and confused, that's progress. You're getting in touch with your feelings. Can you try to write about or draw those feelings?

Don't allow those who hurt you to go on ruining your life!

8

Hanging on to resentment vs. Deciding to let go

For many of us it can be really difficult to stop thinking about "bad" things.

- The way we were treated as a child at home or at school.
- The way our boss treats us.
- Harsh words from family and friends.

What people say...
"Both my sister and I were abused by our father. He always denied it and turned the rest of the family against us. We both tried so hard to forgive him, but he went on and on being so cruel, not even letting our mother meet up with us. When my sister was dying of cancer, I begged Dad to let our mother come. My sister wanted her mother. Dad sent vicious

letters to my sister and she tried to forgive him before she died, but she couldn't.

'God is going to reject me,' my sister said to me, 'because I can't forgive.' So many people told her that if she didn't forgive her father, God would not forgive her.

My lovely sister died in physical and mental pain and I'm so upset that she couldn't die in peace. It was people constantly telling her that she must forgive or God won't forgive her. Now I find it hard to forgive those people. I really try to, but all the time I just keep crying."

Mary

I find people who believe in this kind of condemning God very annoying! It seems so insensitive to say this kind of thing to people who are already struggling with life. Lots of people who believe in God would argue that a God who is merciful and loving would not condemn someone in Mary's sister's position.

Forgiving can be difficult

When people have been traumatized through some awful event that has changed their life for ever, it can be horrendously difficult to forgive those perpetrators, particularly if there is no apology, and no justice.

In those situations, forgiving is made about a billion times more difficult, and it can take many years to work through the process of forgiving to find some sense of peace.

At first, after some outrage – or even cruel words over a cup of tea – we can be left so angry and hurt that any thoughts of forgiving seem impossible. But over a bit of time we can learn to stabilize our feelings and allow life to go on. We can drop our initial anger a little – and find ways to express that safely and creatively. (Helping others, writing, painting, meditating, vigorous exercise, etc.)

What people say...
"The past cannot be changed, so change the future."
   Kay

"Letting go"

Not getting an apology for a "big" event in our lives is a devastating burden to have to carry, whether that's about one individual or a large organization like the local hospital that treated us atrociously. But – and this is the most enormous "but" in the universe – if we don't feel we can or need to forgive, it's very important that we "let go", otherwise:

- the resentment will go on trapping us, keeping us in depression;

- those who hurt us will be going on messing up our life;

- we're likely to go on ruminating about it saying, "If only...";

- we won't be able to make those steps towards finding inner peace and joy.

Being unwilling or unable to "let go" of these negative thoughts is seriously holding us back from healing from depression.

Resentment traps us

There is all the difference in the world between:

- I hate him so much I plan to kill him, and

- I want to "let go", but however much I try, *I can't.*

If you are in that first category and are out for revenge, then, yes, you are likely to stay depressed for a while yet. (But probably over time those feelings of rage will calm a little. Especially if you want that.)

In the second category, you are well on the road to feeling better.

Relax

If you're in that second group, relax. There's no set time for us to "let go" of resentments. Some people take ten seconds to forgive, others need ten years. That's OK.

What's important is that we keep in mind that big question about what kind of person we want to be. If we want to be loving, kind, generous, and so on, we must listen to our inner self and consider how our attitudes today are affecting our long-term plan for our life.

The problem with saying we *won't* "let go" is that we are in danger of allowing our understandable anger to change itself into resentment and bitterness. (If you know anyone who is bitter you will probably agree with me that it makes people awful to be with.)

What people say...
"*It's not my fault, so I'm learning to dump the guilt.*"
  Sally

Strategies for letting go

If you are struggling with "letting go", but want to get rid of the awful feelings you have there are things you can do.

• Just wanting to "let go" is a really good start.

• Many people say that depression is anger turned inwards – rage that we haven't released yet. So if that sounds like you, it might be good to go and see your doctor and ask for help.

First Steps out of Depression

- If that doesn't grab you, I recommend finding lots of old plates and cups and smashing them all into tiny pieces (safely – wear safety goggles!), yelling out your vengeful words. I've done this twice and it was utterly wonderful. Afterwards I felt such peace it amazed me – it was a deeply spiritual experience.

- Get some huge sheets of paper and mix yourself some paint – I always favour lots of black and red – and paint those angry feelings. This can be so releasing it can change your life. (I rather like burning all the painting afterwards and doing a little dance of freedom around the fire.)

"Letting go" is letting our inner spirit turn us towards goodness and love, enabling us to be at peace with ourselves and others.

- Letting go can be hugely difficult – and people who say otherwise are trivializing the whole crucial process of forgiveness in everyone's life.

- Forgiving is not likely to be a one-off event and in a sense we have to forgive every day – whenever we find ourselves ruminating about the person who hurt us.

- It's quite usual to struggle to forgive ourselves.

- I don't think we learn to forgive by beating ourselves up about it.

- I have found freedom from resentment by turning towards the God of Love, and walking in that direction. Yes, that's hard and we fail and stumble. But this is another one of those instances where if we just keep walking, we will get there, one step at a time.

Get back the power!

If we allow those who have hurt us to go on influencing our lives, we are giving those people the power to go on negatively influencing us. *Don't allow that! Turn around!*

Let's get out of here

1. Learn to check when you are ruminating – particularly when you are angry or upset with someone. By the time we've ruminated about a particular person and how much they hurt us, they can metamorphose into a huge monster that is ruining our lives because, we've allowed things to get totally out of proportion.

2. Learn to check who you are blaming for your depression.

If we're saying anything like: "It's all his/her/their fault," we need to take drastic action. (See Chapter 7.)

   Allowing ourselves to become bitter is one sure way to stay in the slough of despond.

Building self-esteem

Hanging on to resentments keeps us in low self-esteem because it keeps us focused on "bad" things.

   We can change that by re-focusing onto something more positive, perhaps by thinking about all the spare space in our brain there will be to do something creative and beautiful instead.

I must confess that I do still ruminate and hang on to some resentments – but every journey begins with a single step. That first step for me is to acknowledge that I'll be a zillion times happier if I "let go".

9

Believing "I'm stuck" vs. Being a creative learner

Most things about depression are hideous. But one thing can in the long run be a creative learning experience for us – we can use that aimless wandering about in the dark to learn to be:

- more of a caring and empathetic person;
- someone who listens to those in pain;
- a "light" to those who are still stuck in the mire.

As we work on finding out what made us depressed, we get insights into who we are as people and it's this information that we need if we are to find an effective route out of the slough of despond – and not fall into it ever again. (Hopefully!)

What people say...
"I don't think I've ever been happy. Not deeply happy like you were talking about."
  Yaz

Yaz said this to me at the end of one of my workshops. She'd told me a bit about the difficult things that had contributed to her depression. She had many reasons to be confused with life, and I could see why she was struggling to experience the contentment and happiness that I think most people seek.

Mythbuster

My life is awful, much worse than anyone else's, and I'm trapped by my past.
This really is the depression talking. These feelings will gradually ease as we journey out of depression.

Choosing happiness?
The idea that happiness is a choice makes no sense at all to us when we are stuck in the mire. The very thought used to anger me. "How can it be about what I choose? Why are some people's lives so happy when I'm stuck in this hell?" I used to moan.

  It took me many years to see that I could choose to be happier, and it was a very long journey to reach a time when I felt deeply happy. Of course, I don't feel that good all the time. But I do now feel content with my life (well, most of the time!) and I work at doing things to make my life even better by, for example, refusing to let myself ruminate.

Talking therapies

At times in my life when I felt "stuck", having therapy was one of the most important things I did. It made my life less terrifying and I discovered:

• what was making me repeatedly depressed;

• that I was both a ruminator and an extremely negative thinker;

• what it was about being alive that freaked me out;

• that I did want to live really, so I could stop thinking I'd like to die;

• that I was an OK person.

But I must admit that every time I've chosen to do some therapy, the whole of my inner world has gone into meltdown. Therapy can start off not too badly, but becomes utterly terrible if we are brave enough to risk talking about our feelings. (There's not much point not being honest with a therapist! That would be near the top of our "most-stupid-things-I-ever-did-in-my-life" list.)

But the good news is that the long-term outcome of risking therapy far outweighs the awfulness. It was like having a baby. The pain was excruciating – but wow! Holding the little one in my arms was joy beyond anything I had ever known.

Therapy is just like that. And, just like babies, it can be mind-bogglingly expensive. So don't make not being able to afford it another reason to get annoyed with the world. Instead, seek out friends and family and tell them you need them to listen to you.

Learning to be content

Striving to make our life better is quite different from that awful characteristic of some people who never seem to be content – ever.

- Instead of rejoicing in life, they push and shove to get more, never content, for example, with what their children achieve. They always want more. And more.
- They make the very worst of everything, angry that their life isn't perfect, and failing to acknowledge that bad things happen to good people.
- However much they have in terms of material possessions or money they always want more.

I think we find love, joy, and peace by learning to be content – and getting out there, contributing something to society.

Mythbuster

I've had too many bad things happen to me ever to be content with my life.
It can be such a struggle to get beyond awful incidents, especially if these have been traumatic, but we can "mend" our lives – gradually – and with love and help from those around us.

Learning to reflect and learn creatively

Over the next few months, as you think about what you have learned through being depressed, you could jot down your key thoughts. These might be something like this:

- Had I not had that time of feeling so low, I might not be able to have those fabulous moments when I can appreciate the beauty of the natural world around me. In those moments I feel so grateful to the Creator God that I'm out of the slough of despond, and glad to be alive.

- Bad things happen to good people. That is just the way the world works, so I need to accept it rather than shouting "It's not fair" and "Why me?"

- Beating myself up just makes a bad situation worse.

- Working through my depression has made me much more self-aware.

Making some rules for life

Being depressed made me much more reflective about my life and I wanted to make myself some rules to live by. I see this as one aspect of having some structure in our lives that psychologists say helps us.

You might want to choose some of your own rules, using this list for ideas:

- Think of life as an adventure.

- Live simply.

- Live in harmony with others.

- Find ways to make your life better.

- Find ways to nurture your inner spirit.

- Find ways to make yourself laugh.

- Look for beauty and wonder in the world.

What people say...
"Live and love in the moment."
  Kay

Finding ourselves

In Willy Russell's film *Educating Rita,* young Rita wants to "find herself". She wants to know about her inner world – about life and what it means. She does this by doing a degree in English Literature, but all of us can be creative learners just by reflecting on our everyday lives – listening to our feelings – and listening (really listening) to others.

I love the bit in the film where Rita sees her mother crying while everyone around them in the pub is smiling and singing.

"There must be a better song to sing than this," her mother says.

Yes, if I take myself back to my teenage years when I was first depressed, I remember so clearly wondering what life was about. Was this it? This awfulness I felt every day at home was intolerable. Do I now just go to school, then get a job to earn money, get beaten up by my husband, and wait till I die? That's what my mother's life seemed to be.

Things we need to know about depression

Being near negative, discontented people isn't good for our own mental health.

Feeling stuck

Being depressed can make us feel stuck in a nightmare. Any God we might have believed in seems to be a tyrant to let us suffer like this. But I think it could be true what people say that whatever happens to each of us through life that is terrible could also be an opportunity for creative learning. (I think this in my more upbeat moods!)

I've certainly learned a huge amount through things I've found tough in my life. Maybe that's just how it is, and we all face difficulties in order to learn what life is about.

I'm so glad that I found a "better song to sing", and it was my experiences of depression that helped me to find it by:

- taking just one step at a time away from the messiness of depression;
- letting my suffering show me that there is meaning and beauty out there in the world;
- letting myself be loved and accepted.

Let's get out of here

Allowing ourselves time to meditate can give us that space in our lives to allow our spiritual selves to seek out a better song to sing.

Building self-esteem

Ultimately it is searching for and finding love that will enable us to see that we are an OK person. We are loved and accepted.

But we need to get "out there" to find it.

✔ It's OK

If you don't feel that you have "found yourself", don't worry. It's something of a life-long quest. Just take the steps you can manage today. That's all any of us can do anyway – just accept that we will be creative learners for the rest of our lives.

10

Choosing despair vs. choosing hope

Despair is deadly. It can be a sign that we're giving up and letting ourselves be dragged even further down into the depths of depression.

Of course, anyone who is depressed is going to have some measure of despair just because that's what depression does. But we *must* push ourselves to reject this darkest of emotions.

- Beg those around you to talk you out of it.

- Look back at photos of happier days.

- Do *anything* but give up and let yourself sink. Maybe watch a favourite film to distract yourself until you can feel the awful despair passing. (This is my absolute favourite strategy for coping when life feels tough.)

One of my favourite films for my worst moments is *Persuasion* and I can allow myself to indulge in the delight of watching Anne Elliot go on and on hoping that Captain Wentworth will fall in love with her again. It often looks as if all hope is lost – but at the last moment he sees that she still loves him, and realizes he still loves her.

Anne's hope explodes into joy! And as I watch this, I have a big grin on my face. *Hope* is fabulous stuff!

What people say...
"Friends and relatives can offer the only effective antidote [to depression] – the 'hope' that such deeply ingrained pessimism is indeed reversible no matter how unlikely that might seem."
Dr James Le Fanu

Choosing hope

Hope is an aspect of life that we might not have thought much about before the Big D got to us – but gradually we learn that it's as effective as the very best antidepressant. It's one of the most crucial things to add to our "map" of how to survive life and travel on our quest to get out of depression and to seek love and happiness.

But hope is quite a slippery idea in some ways, and if you're having trouble thinking what hope might mean to you, try thinking what you might say to yourself in utter despair – then say the opposite. For example:

• "There's no point whatsoever to life and I might as well be dead."

• Answer that with, "There's plenty of point to life! I've made some small changes to my life in the last few weeks and I'm learning that I'm an OK person! I'm getting out of depression, one step at a time."

If you are still unsure what hope is, watch any film where the main character has a problem to solve. For example, in *Star Wars* Luke Skywalker is hoping he can protect his people from the dastardly forces of darkness. Given the technology and number of enemies against him, he really needs to be a hopeful person!

Learning more about depression

I can't tell you everything about depression and the chaos it brings, but when you've taken a few steps, one crucial thing for you to write down is how you felt when the Big D first struck. I call these "early warning signs" and mine are:

- Early morning waking, already anxious, and not wanting the day to start.

- Bursting into tears at the slightest thing and being negative and paranoid (everyone hates me!).

- Not wanting to go out of the house, use the phone or have to meet people.

Your early warning signs might be different because your depression is unique to you – and it is so important to learn to recognize yours.

Our mood is better today

Those days when we know our mood is lifting are so very special. We can take a deep breath – walk to the park and smile because we are much wiser now.

You could write or draw about those wonderful moments so you will remember that:

- depression ends (you could write this on a sticky note to put somewhere obvious)

- and now it is easier to hope.

Your words and drawings will help to remind you of those delicious moments on days when things go wrong and you think you're back in the mire.

Oh no, not again!

The likelihood is, when we feel those early warning signs, we are probably further on the road than we might think. It just *feels* as if we're stuck back where we were long ago. But this time we have:

- the beginnings of a "map" of our inner world;

- some sense of what life is about and where are trying to get to in our life;

- some idea of how to shed light on our innermost feelings;

- a huge amount of self-understanding that we didn't have last time;

- hope, because we know that depression ends. It's choosing to hope rather than allowing ourselves to sink back into despair that can be the final step in knowing we're out of that stinking mire at last.

The journey is a thousand miles, but now we've taken quite a few steps along the way.

Mythbuster

I'm stuck in depression for ever.
No you aren't. Depression ends.

Strategies to keep out of depression

Throughout this book there are a range of strategies to get out, and keep out, of the slough of despond.

- Look back at the "Let's get out of here" headings at the end of chapters.

- Keep on building your self-esteem – especially giving yourself positive messages such as "I am an OK person".

- Make decisions about how you might change your lifestyle. For example, decide to keep a journal so that you are reflecting on your journey, not just meandering along randomly, letting life knock you back into the mire. Or join a self-help group.

- Remember that beating yourself up won't get you anywhere except further into gloom. But nurturing yourself and allowing ourself to indulge in favourite pastimes is an important part of valuing yourself. (One day I'm going to watch the television series *Friends* all the way through.)

- You might want to remind yourself that you need to get out there and not sit at home moping – and watching more television than is good for you!

We must change

From reading this book you have probably worked out that you need to change. That's the key to keeping ourselves free of the Big D. You might want to make a list of the most important things that you've worked out you must change. For example:

- Learning not to turn incidents into catastrophes.

- Working at clarifying boundary issues, especially with "difficult" people.

- Working on "worst-case scenarios" to reduce stress.

- Using the deathbed test.

- Learning to let go of old resentments.

- Making some structure in our lives – lists, rules to live by, etc.

- Teaching ourselves to be content with what we have.

- Learning that it is counterproductive to push ourselves beyond what our body can endure.

- Learning that we can change ourselves, but usually not other people.

Believing in who we are

Being depressed reveals our low self-esteem, and working on building up our inner confidence can have a massive impact on our road to healing.

People who go through self-help programmes, such as the twelve steps of Alcoholics Anonymous, often report that much of their courage and inner strength to stop drinking comes from their belief in a Higher Power.

This same sense of empowerment can come through us meditating and allowing ourselves to marvel at the beauty around us. There is something so enlivening about the natural world. One snowdrop comes out in early spring and I feel a thousand times more cheerful.

There *is* meaning out there beyond the daily grind – beyond those weird and awful times when all we can do is sit and cry.

I hope this book has shown you that:

- some things sap us of our inner power (all that negative thinking);

- things such as the activities in this book, meditating and focusing on beautiful and creative things, can empower us and transform how we think and how we feel;

- we *can* search for love, joy, contentment and peace of mind – and we *can* find all those things if we get out there rather than sit at home waiting for it all to come to us. Those who sit and wait for love to fall into their lap might have a really long wait.

It's likely that even if you've worked your way through the

whole book, life still feels a terrible struggle. That's why I made it a "dip into" book so that you can go back again and again to bits that you know you didn't quite grasp first time around.

I hope by reading this book you will see that you are not alone. Others have taken those steps away from depression before you and have walked the path to find love, joy, and peace.

Our inner power

A great film moment for me is at the end of *Star Wars* episode four when Luke Skywalker has only a few seconds to blow up the Death Star and save everyone from the evil destructive armies. Obi-Wan Kenobi's voice comes to Luke reminding him to trust in his "inner force".

Trusting in our inner spirit and drawing on a Higher Power will help us through life's journey – and enable us to smile along the way.

The God of Love be with you as you travel on....

...and remember that great truth of life: *depression ends*!

 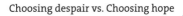

For the family

It can be perplexing and demanding for the rest of the family if one member is depressed. These are some pointers to what can be most useful for the depressed person. But remember, rather a lot of the time, whatever you do, they are going to say you get it "wrong"!

1. Listen to them – be supportive and reassuring. Allowing them to talk helps them work through their problems.

2. Don't take on too much. You might find it painful and emotionally demanding to hear what they say.

3. Try not to interrupt, even when they are saying things you think are untrue. ("Everyone hates me", for example.)

4. Try not to jump in and give advice. It's you listening that is important and if you can try to identify with what they are feeling, and maybe reflect some of that back at them (for example, "I can hear your sadness and confusion") this is likely to be hugely supportive because they will feel less alone, and that someone understands their pain.

5. Don't say things like "Pull yourself together". They would if they could – but they can't.

6. Take care of your own needs and those of the rest of the

family and friends. Selfishness is common in depressed people but this is likely to diminish as they get better.

7. Look out for signs that they are suicidal. Make sure you, and the one you love, know an emergency 24-hour helpline number or email. (See Useful Resources.) Put the information where you can both see it. You might just have to ask, "Are you feeling that life might not be worth living?" It's best to let them talk about their suicidal feelings – but this is likely to be distressing for both of you. If you feel a crisis coming or you feel you need help, take them to the doctor or the hospital emergency department. You might want to make sure there aren't large quantities of drugs, such as paracetamol, antidepressants or tranquillizers, in the house. However if someone you love does kill themselves, it is not your fault. The responsibility rests with the depressed person.

8. They might be glad if you could accompany them to their doctor. (It's crucial that they see a doctor.) But don't take over and talk for them. Reassure them that medical treatment does work and they will get better.

9. Try to remain hopeful – the depression will end.

Useful Resources

Make sure you know an emergency helpline.

UK   08457 909090

If you are in crisis, you can ring the Samaritans day or night.
Tel: 08457 909090.
Website: www.samaritans.org

New Zealand   0800 543354

For 24-hour telephone counselling, contact LifeLine New Zealand.
Tel: 0800 543354
Website: www.lifeline.co.nz

Australia   13 11 14

For 24-hour telephone counselling at the cost of a local call, ring Lifeline.
Tel: 13 11 14
Website: www.lifeline.org.au